May 1967

RS 3434/7
ABC ATOMIC WEAPON DATA
Sigma

HISTORY OF GUN-TYPE BOMBS AND WARHEADS (W)

Mks 8, 10 and 11 (U) *Title unclassified per Susan Stinchcomb 4/18/2002*

SC-H-67-658

BEST AVAILABLE COPY

Redacted Version

Information Research Division, 3434

THIS DOCUMENT CONSISTS OF __60 PAGES

Classified By: Richard B. Craner
Classification Analyst, Org 4225
Date: 12/12/2007
Derived From: TCG-NAS-2, 03/97, DOE OC

63 pgs

THE TX-8 BOMB

Mk 8 Exterior View

RS 3434/7

(b)(1), (b)(3)

LENGTH—116 IN.

DIAMETER—14.5 IN.

WEIGHT—3150 LBS

Mk 8 Cross Section

Timetable of Weapon Events

<u>Mk 8 Bomb</u>

7/25/46   Bikini Baker shot in Operation Crossroads sparks request that an
            underwater detonation weapon be considered.

1946-47   Z Division studies possibility of creating a penetrating bomb.

5/15/47   Weapons Subcommittee of the General Advisory Committee of the
            Atomic Energy Commission postpones consideration of a penetrating
            weapon.

10/2/47   Committee on Atomic Energy recommends that facilities of the Bureau
            of Ordnance be used in the study of a gun-type penetrating weapon.

4/9/48   Military Liaison Committee requests Atomic Energy Commission to
            undertake development of a penetrating weapon, using Bureau of
            Ordnance facilities.

7/48   Code name of LC (Elsie) assigned to project.

11/18/49   Sandia is assigned design responsibilities in the Elsie program.

4/50   Ordnance Division C established to centralize Sandia design
            responsibilities in the Elsie program.

8/30/50   Sandia is assigned production responsibilities for Elsie, now
            renamed the TX-8 Bomb.

10/3/50   Division of Military Application restricts development of
            externally carried TX-8 to subsonic aircraft.

11/10/50   Desired military and technical characteristics of penetrating-type
            weapons issued.

| 12/8/50 | TX-G Steering Committee appointed and holds initial meeting. |

1/20/51 (b)(3)

3/15/51

Early 1951 — Externally carried TX-8 Bomb assigned nomenclature of TX-8 Prime.

10/51 — TX-8 Prime program divided into two parts: TX-8-X1 (to cover carriage at subsonic speeds) and TX-8-X2 (a program to reduce drag in high-speed carriage).

11/51 — Mk 8 Mod 0 achieves production.

1/52 — Mk 8 Mod 0 enters stockpile.

4/1/52 (b)(3)

9/53 — Mk 8 Bomb with Mk 8 Mod 1 Fuze (TX-8-X2) enters stockpile.

11/55 — Mk 8 Mod 3 Bomb enters stockpile.

5/57 — Mk 8 Bombs retired as Mk 11 enters stockpile.

Mk 8 Warhead

3/50 — Gun-type warheads considered for missile application.

9/13/50 — Santa Fe Operations Office requests that penetrating warheads be applied to guided missiles.

2/14/51 — Santa Fe Operations Office authorizes design of XW-8/REGULUS.

1/18/52 — XW-5/REGULUS program assigned priority over XW-8/REGULUS.

8/21/52 — Field Command forwards proposed military characteristics for XW-8/REGULUS to Sandia.

9/24/53 — Successful XW-8/REGULUS system test held.

-6-   RS 3434/7

8/54   Design of XW-8/REGULUS completed.

5/20/55   Program activity suspended.

TX-10 Weapon

5/6/48   Sandia Research and Development Board assigns priorities to
              weapon design projects.

1/21/49   Division of Military Application requests Bureau of Ordnance to
              study possible adaptation of Mk 8 as a light air-burst weapon.

4/22/49   Military Liaison Committee requests that study be restricted to
              a preliminary investigation.

3/8/50   Guided-missile symposium at Sandia Base proposes use of a light-
              weight gun-type device as a missile warhead.

7/6/50   Military Liaison Committee releases formal requirement for an
              air-burst, gun-type warhead.

8/9/50   Military Liaison Committee establishes formal requirement for
              a lightweight air-burst bomb.

8/17/50   Division of Military Application forwards characteristics for
              lightweight air-burst bombs.

9/6/50   Bureau of Ordnance, in reply to January 21, 1949 request of the
              Division of Military Application, offers to adapt the Mk 8 as a
              lightweight air-burst bomb.

10/3/50   Division of Military Application notifies Bureau of Ordnance that
              Sandia will develop the lightweight air-burst bomb.

10/18/50   Sandia Weapons Development Board discusses bomb and warhead
              applications. Santa Fe Operations Office subsequently authorizes
              deletion of warhead requirement. Bomb officially designated the
              TX-10.

12/14/50	TX-G Committee discusses TX-10, comparing its design with the TX-7, and recommends that the TX-10 be terminated.
12/20/50	Sandia Weapons Development Board accepts recommendations of TX-G Committee.
2/12/51	Division of Military Application recommends cancellation of TX-10 program. Military Liaison Committee requests its continuance at low priority.
4/10/51	TX-10 design status reviewed by Sandia Weapons Development Board. Design found not to meet desired military characteristics, and project returned to the study phase.
5/7/52	Military Liaison Committee reports TX-10 project canceled by Joint Chiefs of Staff.

Mk 11 Weapon

3/50	Guided-missile meetings at Sandia Base. Gun-type devices considered for warhead application.
4/17/50	Department of Defense proposes desired military and technical characteristics of impact, delayed-action-type atomic bombs.
7/31/50	Division of Military Application requests Bureau of Ordnance to design a Mk 8-type bomb for external carriage on high-speed aircraft.
11/29/50	Nomenclature of TX-11 assigned to weapon.
7/24/51	Sandia requests Bureau of Ordnance to adapt TX-11 design for warhead application.
8/6/51	Desired military characteristics of Mk 11 issued.
6/52	Warhead application for Mk 11 deleted.
Mid-1954	Production version of TX-11 named the Mk 91 Mod 0 Bomb.

RS 3434/7

4/1/55   Mk 11 design released.

~~SECRET RESTRICTED DATA~~

1/1/56   Early production units of Mk 11 (Mk 91 Mod 0) become available.

7/1/56   Mk 91 Mod 0 enters stockpile.

8/56

(b)(3)

~~SECRET RESTRICTED DATA~~ UNCLASSIFIED

History of Gun-Type Bombs and Warheads

Mk 8 Bomb

The gun method of assembling nuclear material, used in the wartime Little Boy
design, was the first atomic weapon system to be devised, predating the estab-
lishment of the Los Alamos Laboratory. The method was nuclearly inefficient
and was largely ignored for a time after the end of World War II, while interest
centered on implosion techniques.

(b)(1), (b)(3)

At this time, the Los Alamos Scientific Laboratory was fully occupied in the
above-mentioned study of improvements in implosion devices, and suggested that
the task of developing a water-penetrating weapon (which probably would use gun
techniques) could best be accomplished by a military group. No immediate action
was taken on this suggestion, but the subject was briefly examined by the Z
Division of Los Alamos in late 1946 and early 1947.

(b)(1), (b)(3)

The topic was
subsequently discussed in a meeting of the Weapons Subcommittee of the AEC General
Advisory Committee, and a decision made May 15, 1947 that consideration of a
penetrating weapon be postponed.[4]

Meanwhile, however, the Military Liaison Committee had been discussing the general
subject of subsurface atomic weapons. At the instigation of the Navy member,
Rear Admiral William S. Parsons (who had armed the wartime gun-type Little Boy for

its historic drop on Hiroshima), Section ReM of the Navy's Bureau of Ordnance, prepared preliminary sketches of a penetrating gun device.

At about the same time, other groups were considering the same subject. The Joint Research and Development Board had established a Committee on Atomic Energy, and the subject of penetrating weapons was discussed in the October 2, 1947 meeting of this Committee. It was urged that serious consideration be given to the development of a gun-type device suitable for penetration use. Since the AEC weapon laboratories were already fully occupied with other high-priority work, the Committee recommended that the facilities of the Bureau of Ordnance be used.[5]

The Division of Military Application had also been considering the advisability of invoking the assistance of the military services in the development of penetrating weapons. Los Alamos had noted that gun systems were inherently inefficient, and expressed an opinion that the weapons laboratories should continue to concentrate on design of implosion devices.[6] Thus the Military Liaison Committee was requested to assign mechanical design of a gun-type penetration weapon to the Bureau of Ordnance.[7]

These several requests, all in the same vein, were presented for consideration to the Military Liaison Committee which, April 9, 1948, requested the Atomic Energy Commission to undertake development of a penetrating-type weapon, using the facilities of the Bureau of Ordnance.[8] This request was formally presented to the Bureau April 27, 1948, and accepted.[9] A code name of "Minnie" was initially assigned to the project, but was later found to have been used for a Bureau of Ships propulsion project and, in mid-July 1948, the name was changed to "LC" (a follow-on term to "LB," for the Little Boy), and which came to be commonly written as "Elsie."[10] That the Elsie program was considered a matter of some interest to the Military was indicated in a May 6, 1948 meeting of the Sandia Research and Development Board in which the project was assigned top priority, second only to the schedule for getting the Mk 4 Bomb into full-scale production.

The Bureau of Ordnance issued detailed work assignments. The Naval Ordnance Laboratory would be responsible for developing suitable pyrotechnic delay fuzes.

The Naval Ordnance Test Station would study external ballistics and design the tail. The Naval Powder Factory would investigate powder development. The Naval Ordnance Plant would handle much of the manufacturing and testing program, and when this location was subsequently closed, the work would be transferred to the Naval Proving Grounds and the Naval Gun Factory. Section ReM of the Bureau of Ordnance would provide overall design controls, including the task of guaranteeing survival of the nuclear assembly under impact conditions.

The development program would proceed in three overlapping phases. Feasibility and preliminary design studies would outline the most promising general design characteristics of the weapon, and these were scheduled for completion January 1, 1949. The second phase, covering experimental development and testing of proto-type weapon design, would be completed a year later. The third phase, manufacture of prototype weapons, would be finished in another year, or January 1, 1951.

(b)(3)

The studies advanced rapidly and, by September 3, 1948, the Bureau of Ordnance could report that the design appeared feasible and that a weapon could probably be devised that would function satisfactorily after impact on water, and possibly after impact on hard surfaces which the weapon might encounter beneath the surface of the water.[11] It was initially felt that the fuze should be actuated at impact and have a delay of 1 to 2 minutes before bomb detonation, but it was later decided that a more reliable bomb would be created if the fuze action were initiated at time of release of the bomb from the carrying aircraft.

The diameter of the bomb would be about 14 inches and the weight would be about 3000 pounds, as compared to 28 inches and 8900 pounds for the Little Boy. These reductions were due to the more compact nuclear assembly and a decrease in the thickness of the bomb case. The shape would be roughly cylindrical, with a flat nose for good penetration characteristics, and the bomb would attain a maximum impact velocity of 1500 feet per second. The minimum release altitude would be 500 feet, to give the bomb enough time during its fall to assume proper entry attitude, and there would be no restriction on maximum release altitude. It was felt that three separate and independent fuzes should be used, to provide adequate reliability. A meeting was held October 25 and 26, 1948, with Los Alamos assuming the task of developing impact-resistant initiators.[12]

An extensive series of tests was performed. The first group included 174 half-scale bombs of 6.25-inch diameter. These were fabricated in 49 different configurations, and were impacted against targets of steel and concrete at different angles, striking velocities, and missile temperatures ranging from -65°F to +165°F.

(b)(3)

Following the above, some 38 full-scale impact tests were conducted, to confirm the half-scale results. Interior ballistic tests were performed, to check the burning rate of various propellants and the behavior of the missile in the gun barrel. As fuze components became available, they were subjected to the shock produced by firing from a 14.25-inch-diameter railway gun.

Two series of wind-tunnel tests were held, one at the University of Minnesota to obtain aerodynamic coefficients of various tail configurations, and the other at the California Institute of Technology Cooperative Wind Tunnel to evaluate aerodynamic characteristics of five basic designs.

Airplane drop tests were made of 109 5-inch tailless models at different water-entry angles. The best nose shape thus developed was given 21 additional tests with varying afterbody configurations. Six complete 5-inch models were dropped from an altitude of 15,000 feet, and 26 full-scale bombs were subjected to water-entry tests produced by a variable-angle launcher at the Morris Dam Torpedo Range.

When complete sets of internal components became available, 39 prototypes were dropped, to verify component functioning. Impact tests against various combinations of concrete and steel targets were conducted on 20 prototypes, as well as low- and high-temperature environmental tests.

Up to this point, Sandia had not been concerned with the Elsie. The Atomic Energy Act of 1946, however, stated that the Atomic Energy Commission was responsible for manufacturing and stockpiling of atomic weapons, and now that production appeared imminent, it was necessary to bring the AEC weapon laboratories into the picture. On November 18, 1949, the Division of Military Application proposed that Sandia enter the program by designing the airplane release mechanism, conducting drop tests at Salton Sea Test Base, establishing reliability criteria for the arming and firing system of the Elsie, designing test and handling equipment, and providing training for the military field teams that were to handle the bomb.[13] This proposal was accepted by Sandia February 1, 1950,[14] and Ordnance Division C was established in April 1950, to centralize Sandia's responsibilities in the program.[15]

A conference was held at the Naval Ordnance Test Station June 18-19, 1950. It was reported that external ballistics were being checked on a full-size prototype bomb and that the drops were confirming wind-tunnel results. The ballistic features were excellent; water entry was satisfactory, with no broaching being apparent even at extreme angles (84 degrees) from the normal. A case had been built of alloy steel and was performing satisfactorily in tests against concrete at impact veloci-ties of 1500 feet per second, the maximum that the Elsie would be expected to attain in a high-altitude drop.

With the outbreak of hostilities in Korea in mid-1950, plans for producing Elsie weapons were accelerated, and a desired stockpile data of July 1951 was established.[16] A decision was made to assign full production responsibility to Sandia, and this

directive was issued August 30, 1950, accompanied by a request that the facilities of the Bureau of Ordnance be used to the fullest extent possible.[17]   At
this time, the Elsie was assigned nomenclature of TX-8.[18]

An intensive study had been undertaken of changes required to allow external
carriage of the TX-8. There were several reasons why these changes were necessary.
For one, the fuze system had been designed to operate under protected bomb-bay
conditions. For another, the shape of the TX-8, with its blunt nose, caused
excessive drag, especially at high speeds.

(b)(3)

It was obvious that this
would require considerable study, and it was suggested that the Bureau of Ordnance
establish a parallel program for the development of a Mk II Elsie suitable for
either internal or external suspension, while work continued on an internally
carried TX-8.[19]

The Bureau made a survey and reported that the existing shape of the TX-8 was
adequate for subsonic external carriage if some minor changes were made to the
tail design,[20] and the shape could be carried in the space available under the
centerline of the F4U, AD and A2D airplanes. It was noted that development of a
shape for external carriage at supersonic velocities would require additional
study and development, and this effort would be of interest in connection with a
recent proposal that an XW-8 Warhead be fitted to a guided missile. Subsequently,
October 3, 1950, the Division of Military Application authorized development of an
externally carried TX-8 with subsonic aircraft and development of a new bomb (the
TX-11) for high-speed external carriage.[21]

Meanwhile, the Armed Forces Special Weapons Project had been drawing up a paper
specifying the desired military and technical characteristics of penetrating-type
weapons.

(b)(1), (b)(3)

This paper was circulated for comment to Sandia and Los Alamos as well as the Military, and was subjected to a critical review.[23] The formal issue of the characteristics on November 10, 1950, however, retained the release speed requirement and noted that the bomb should function reliably when released at any altitude up to 50,000 feet and survive impacts on water, reinforced concrete, and--hopefully--thin steel plate.

(b)(3)

The November 22, 1950 meeting of the Sandia Weapons Development Board reviewed the overall gun-type weapons program, which now included the TX-9, TX-10, and TX-11, in addition to the TX-8. It was noted that the TX-8 was composed of three main parts: The nose, the tail, and the clamping ring which joined them. The bomb diameter had been fixed at 14.5 inches, its length at 116 inches, and its weight at 3260 pounds. The nose was a heavy forging with a blunt shape for water and ground entry, and contained the internal gun barrel, tamper, and projectile.

(b)(3)

A saddle on the external top of the bomb case contained switches and electrical connections to operate the primers.[25]

Sandia had proposed that an interlaboratory gun-type weapon coordination committee be established, similar in scope and authority to the TX-5 Steering Committee. Action was taken on this suggestion in late 1950, and the first meeting of this Gun Committee, with representation from Los Alamos and Sandia, was held December 8, 1950.[26] At this time, the TX-5 Steering Committee was renamed the TX-N Steering Committee to reflect its interest in all implosion weapons, and the new Gun Committee came to be known as the TX-G Steering Committee.

The first meeting of the TX-G Committee heard a report from Los Alamos concerning progress on design of an initiator for the TX-8. The initial design had been based on the device used in the Little Boy, and was then modified as design weaknesses were uncovered by the testing program. Some idea of the problems encountered were shown by the increasing impact requirements as the design progressed. The initial assumption had been that the highest shock encountered in ground impact would be 7500 g's. This figure had progressively increased during design and was now 100,000 to 300,000 g's.

(b)(3)

Studies were meanwhile in progress on systems for nuclear safing.

(b)(3)

In early 1951 it was decided to identify the adaptation of the TX-8 for external carriage at subsonic speeds as the TX-8' (or TX-8 Prime) program. Plans were made to make only minor changes to the TX-8 and provide early, but only partial, satisfaction of the requirements for an externally carried TX-8. It was felt that, if this program could not be accomplished within a short time, it should be canceled in favor of the TX-11 Bomb, then being designed for external carriage on high-speed aircraft.

At this time, the AD4 and the F4U5 were the only carriers specified for the TX-8'. The AD4 was selected as the test aircraft, and Sandia issued a contract through the Bureau of Aeronautics to Douglas Aircraft Company to modify this aircraft for TX-8 carriage. Douglas designed a nose cap to reduce drag and help protect the TX-8' fuzing elements.

Sandia issued Report SC1936(TR), An Evaluation of the TX-8' (Externally Carried Mark 8 Weapon), July 1, 1951. This reported that the feasibility of delivering the weapon externally on attack aircraft had been successfully demonstrated and that subsequent tests on fighter airplanes could be expected to meet with similar success.[29] Sandia recommended that the TX-8' program be authorized for full development, as it was felt that the weapon would be available far enough ahead of the TX-11 to be of use to the Military.[30]

The above proposal was considered by the Sandia Weapons Development Board in a meeting August 8, 1951. It was noted that the adaptation of the TX-8 initiation and suspension system (called, in Navy parlance, the T-28 saddle) had proved that little buffeting and restriction of aircraft performance could be expected at speeds up to and including the top safe speed of the AD4 aircraft, or Mach 0.72. Meanwhile, the F2H aircraft had been suggested as a carrier for the TX-8', and the time required to complete the bomb development would depend on the availability of this aircraft. A T-31 system, suitable for use with faster aircraft, would not be available for another 6 months.[31]

Tests had meanwhile been made of the possibility of "cook-off" or explosion of bomb fuzes in a fire caused by crash of the aircraft. These tests showed that the fuze primers would become ignited in about 5 minutes in almost any type of fire, while ignition of the main propellant charge would take somewhat longer. This provided a reasonable margin of safety for pilot escape from the burning wreckage. Additionally, impact tests against concrete targets had demonstrated that the fuzes were unlikely to explode through mere impact. Thus it was decided that the tape which retracted the interrupter in the nose fuz (this fuze was recessed deeply into the weapon case) would be permanently attached to the aircraft and pulled out at each drop. The side fuze tapes could be pulled or dropped in safed condition, at the option of the crew of the carrying aircraft.

The Division of Military Application approved the TX-8' program September 10, 1951, and directed that Sandia proceed with the design.[32] The project was restricted to compatibility of the bomb with the AD4 airplane and the T-28 saddle.

-18- RS 3434/7

In late October 1951, the TX-8' program was divided into two parts; the TX-8-X1 and TX-8-X2. The X1 was the basic TX-8' program; the X2 was to provide a cleaner aerodynamic design and reduce the drag caused by the saddle. Inasmuch as 20 drops had already been made with the TX-8-X1, its compatibility and reliability were felt to have been proven, and attention was concentrated on the TX-8-X2 design.[33]

The T-28 saddle functions were replaced by a small box located in the aircraft fuselage. This allowed the use of a standard two-hook bomb rack and increased the clearance between the externally carried bomb and the ground. Fairings were installed over the side fuzes to reduce drag. Fuze tapes used for safing were pulled through the nose fairing to protect them from the windstream. A quick disconnect was installed, to permit the weapon to be dropped with tapes in place, thus leaving barriers in the path between the primer and the propellant, and preventing the fuzes from firing the main propellant charge.

This new device was called the T-31, and a subcontract was issued for its development. Due to the subsequent failure of the subcontractor to achieve a satisfactory T-31, Sandia produced a design having the T-31 located inside the bomb pylon, thus making it possible to detach the arming tapes from the pylon after bomb release, and prevent aircraft damage caused by whipping of the tapes in the slipstream. This work was undertaken November 5, 1951, and satisfactory hardware was being produced 10 days later.

The Mk 8 Mod 0 weapon was initially produced in November 1951 and was stockpiled in January 1952.

(b)(1), (b)(3)

(b)(1), (b)(3)

Early drop tests of the TX-8-X2 from the F2H aircraft resulted in severe pitching at time of separation from the aircraft.[34] This was caused by air loading resulting from a nose-down attitude of the bomb with respect to the aircraft, and was corrected by use of an ejection system plus a tail revision, in which three fins replaced the circular shroud of the initial design.[35]

A nose cap of frangible material was tested in low-altitude drops, both with the AD4 and the F2H. Good ground entry was achieved in all cases, with the frangible cap having no adverse effect on penetration. Water drops were made at the Salton Sea Test Base from the relatively low altitude of 150 feet and an air speed of 260 knots. These drops resulted in excellent water entry at angles of 10 degrees, with no ricochet or broaching of the bomb.

(b)(3)

The Sandia Weapons Development Board met April 16, 1952. Two problems were raised by the Military; weapon propellant temperature limitations, and possible leakage of water into the interior of the gun barrel of the Mk 8.[38]

(b)(3)

An upper limit of 90°F for long-term storage was accordingly established, with a 24-hour limitation at 160°F. Subsequently, the long-term storage temperature was raised to 120°F, but installation of the propellant in the breech plug was not to be made prior to 24 hours before a mission, as physical compression of the propellant increased the bonding action.

The Military Liaison Committee, in a letter dated October 20, 1952, requested
that the bomb be designed to withstand storage for 6-month periods under
occasional temperature extremes of -80°F to +165°F, and flight bomb-bay temperatures of -90°F. It was pointed out that external bomb carriage might experience
even more rigorous conditions of -100°F during a 12-hour flight, and that the
24-hour limitation regarding weapon assembly would be operationally troublesome.[40]

Inasmuch as the propellant characteristics were specified by the Bureau of Ordnance,
the problem was referred to this organization.[41] It was noted that the environmental
criteria had been specified after detail design of the Mk 8 had been essentially
completed, and that these criteria differed considerably from the initial Mk 8
development objectives. It was also pointed out that any project to provide a
propellant with improved temperature characteristics would duplicate work being
undertaken in the TX-11 program. The Bureau of Ordnance subsequently allowed
relaxation of the temperature limitations to 7 days at 130°F, 60 days at 120°F, and
indefinitely at 110°F.[42] On March 12, 1953, the Military Liaison Committee agreed
that major redesign efforts toward relieving temperature limits be directed toward
the TX-11.[43]

The possibility of water leakage into the interior of the gun nuclear system had
been a matter of early concern.

(b)(1), (b)(3)   When recovered,
there was only about half a cup of water in the barrel, and this leakage was not
felt great. Nevertheless, the Military, in the April 16, 1952 meeting of the
Sandia Weapons Development Board, requested that the possible effects of this
leakage on weapon performance be studied.[38]

Consequently, drops were made on a limestone bed in southwestern New Mexico.
This rock possessed extremely high compressive strengths, from 18,000 to 23,000
pounds per square inch (average concrete strengths were about 4500 psi).

(b)(1), (b)(3)

Only one weapon showed any evidence of leakage. Experiments were
started, using O-rings as replacements for the cork gaskets used to seal the open-
ings in the bomb case.

It had been decided that the TX-8-X2 changes constituted a modification to the fuze rather than the bomb. Thus the Mk 8 Bomb with Mk 8 Mod 1 Fuze, incorporating a frangible nose and T-31 fuze tape control, was released for production and entered stockpile September 1953.

The TX-G Committee, whose functions had been largely assumed by the Special Weapons Development Board, was dissolved in January 1954. The Aspen Committee, which was directing Sandia-Los Alamos activities on the TX-11 weapon, agreed to handle any residual interlaboratory matters on the Mk 8 program.

(b)(3)

' This change was made in the Mk 8 Mod 2 Bomb which was stockpiled in May 1955.

Meanwhile, studies had been made of the desirability of replacing the original Abner initiator with an improved design, the Phoebe. This change, plus the O-rings for sealing the bomb case, was known as the TX-8-X3 program during development.[44] Changes to the Atomic Energy Act permitted the Military to produce and stockpile certain atomic weapons parts, and it was suggested that the Bureau of Ordnance assume control of TX-8-X3 production work.[45] This proposal was rejected by the Atomic Energy Commission, which felt that close phasing was required, due to changes to both nuclear and nonnuclear portions of the Mk 8, and that Sandia should retain production control.[46] The Mk 8 Mod 3 was stockpiled in October 1955.

By February 1957, the Mk 11 Bomb was in production and entering stockpile. A decision was made to retire the Mk 8 weapons on a one-for-one basis as Mk 11's entered War Reserve. This retirement program started May 1957 and was completed 2 months later.

Mk 8 Warhead

The first consideration of a gun-type device for use with guided missiles was in a Los Alamos meeting of early March 1950, in which various missile programs were discussed.[47] Little immediate action was taken and, during the summer of that year, attention was concentrated on developing the Elsie as a free-fall bomb to be released from aircraft. However, September 13, 1950, Santa Fe Operations Office requested Sandia and Los Alamos to consider the application of a penetrating warhead to various guided missiles. The missiles suggested were the HERMES A-3, HERMES C-1, REGULUS, RIGEL, and TRITON.[48]

It was obvious that a gun-type warhead would be more impact-resistant than an implosion design, and the request was referred to the Bureau of Ordnance, then doing work on the Mk 8 Bomb.

(b)(1), (b)(3)

Any missile usage would involve higher impact velocities and require new tests and additional design effort.[49] The Division of Military Application then referred the project to the Sandia Weapons Development Board, requesting that any Mk 8 Warhead developed be compatible with the above five missiles.[50]

Sandia made a preliminary study and, December 20, 1950, reported to the Santa Fe Operations Office that a firm estimate of the magnitude of the program could not be made. The terminal velocities of the missiles cited had not been definitely fixed, but were believed to be significantly greater than any previously considered in atomic-bomb design. Sandia proposed that a general investigation of impact warheads be continued, in an effort to delineate the most universally useful type of warhead and to outline a development program.[51]

The Santa Fe Operations Office suggested that initial application of the penetrating warhead be made to the REGULUS missile. This missile, scheduled for production in 1953, had a comparatively low impact velocity, and it was felt that a suitable warhead might be created by relatively simple modifications of existing components.[52] Sandia reported, January 23, 1951, that the development of such a warhead appeared feasible, and that the Bureau of Ordnance had been requested to investigate the effects of impact velocities and warhead mounting methods on the penetration characteristics of the Mk 8 device.[53]

The XW-8/REGULUS was authorized for design activity by the Santa Fe Operations Office February 14, 1951.[54] It was noted that since the REGULUS would attain an

RS 3434/7

impact velocity of only Mach 1.2, there would be few shock problems, unless the weapon were employed against extremely hard targets such as igneous rock or heavy armor plate.[55]

It was determined that the fuzing accuracy for the XW-8/REGULUS could be less than for an air-burst device, since the only requirement was to initiate a pyrotechnic delay train about one minute prior to impact. Should the weapon be launched from a submarine, a simple arming system would protect the submarine against premature detonations.

The Sandia Weapons Development Board discussed the Mk 8 missile-warhead program in its April 10, 1951 meeting. It was felt that current weapon capabilities would not allow impact velocities higher than Mach 2.5 without danger of breakup of the device. Since the terminal velocity of the HERMES was estimated to be Mach 4.5, it was obvious that radical changes to either warhead or missile would have to be made if this missile were used. It was apparent that either approach would require much design investigation, and it was decided to consider only the XW-8/REGULUS.[56]

It was found that the warhead compartment of the REGULUS was long enough to hold the basic Mk 8 Bomb assembly, but that little excess clearance was available, and that access to the nose of the weapon was difficult. Additionally, the center of gravity of the missile would be about 30 inches forward of its optimum location, and it was decided to delete the afterbody of the Mk 8. Tests were started to determine the terraballistics of the Mk 8 without its afterbody, and to ascertain whether the warhead would break away from the missile on impact with various surfaces.[57]

Another problem was the development of a mechanism to ignite the propellant of the internal gun device of the XW-8/REGULUS. In the drop bomb, this was accomplished by arming tapes, but the warhead application required either a device to pull the tapes at the proper point in the missile trajectory or a modification of the fuze.

Work had meanwhile been proceeding on the design of an XW-5 Warhead for the
REGULUS and, on January 18, 1952, the Navy requested that this application be
given priority. This was not to preclude concurrent work on the XW-8 application, but to ensure that the XW-5 design had first consideration in the event of
conflicting requirements.[58]

By February 26, 1952, the Bureau of Ordnance had completed its study of the
XW-8/REGULUS and proposed two fuze designs.

(b)(3)

Some attention had been given to an XW-11/REGULUS weapon, since
the design limits on the XW-11 were higher than those of the Mk 8. The Bureau
requested, however, that emphasis be placed on the XW-8/REGULUS, since the early
TX-11 tests had indicated that extensive warhead redesign might be required.[59]

The Division of Military Application subsequently notified the Military Liaison
Committee, April 1, 1952, that the Mk 8 nuclear system would be adapted to the
REGULUS, and the TX-11 design reserved for missiles with higher impact velocities.
Tests had shown that the XW-8 Warhead could survive REGULUS impact speeds, but
that other missiles had impact speeds that substantially exceeded even the
capability of the XW-11.[60]

The Ad Hoc Working Group for the XW-5/REGULUS was requested to provide a fuze
for the XW-8/REGULUS.[61] The Group could not decide whether this work should be
done by the Bureau of Ordnance or Sandia, and referred the problem to the Guided
Missiles Committee.[62] This Committee recommended to the Special Weapons Development Board that the Navy be responsible for the transmission of any radio command
signals to the missile and for the reception of these signals in the missile, and
that Sandia be responsible for applying these signals to the warhead installation
to cause arming or safing.[63] Under this recommendation, which was approved, Sandia
became responsible for the entire warhead installation, including mounting structure,
terraballistic tail, and arming and fuzing system components.

The proposed military characteristics for the XW-8/REGULUS were forwarded by Field
Command to Sandia August 21, 1952. The warhead would have a diameter of 14-1/2
inches, a length of 63.85 inches, and a weight of about 3050 pounds. The warhead

yield would be the same as that of the Mk 8 Bomb. The warhead would function
properly when subjected to missile impact speeds up to Mach 1.1 on water, earth,
reinforced concrete and, if possible, harder targets. It would not broach or
ricochet after impacts at angles between 60 and 90 degrees. The weapon would
penetrate the target and detonate after coming to rest, and would be sufficiently
watertight to function after water impact, followed by bottom impact.[64]

The Military Liaison Committee notified the Division of Military Application,
October 3, 1952, that no requirement existed for design of penetration warheads
capable of impact velocities higher than those of the REGULUS missile.[65]

Meanwhile, the Military decided that efficient use of the XW-8/REGULUS weapon
required a high delivery accuracy. This was not possible with the existing
missile system, and production requirements were deferred, awaiting refinement
of the missile guidance system. Sandia was requested to complete its design
work on the warhead, and the Navy was asked to proceed with scheduled flight
tests.[66]

Successful component evaluation flights were conducted, and a successful warhead
system test was held September 24, 1953. The Military Liaison Committee then
suggested that, since there were few differences between the XW-8 Warhead and the
extensively tested Mk 8 Bomb, further systems tests be held in abeyance.[67]

Design of the missile-warhead was completed in August 1954, and Report SC3483(TR),
Status and Evaluation of the XW-8/REGULUS Warhead Installation at Design Release,
was presented to the December 1, 1954 meeting of the Special Weapons Development
Board.[68] The warhead was named the Mk 8 Mod 2, and production responsibility
assigned to the Bureau of Ordnance.

The warhead contained three delay fuzes, two located on the side and one on the
nose.
(b)(3)

All requirements of the military characteristics were satisfied by the test program, although impact tests at less than 90 degrees were not conducted, and it was

not definitely determined whether the warhead would penetrate the target or break away on impact. However, Mk 8 Bomb tests had shown that satisfactory penetrations were achieved at entry angles as low as 30 degrees to the surface, and it was felt that the warhead would have similar satisfactory characteristics.

Subsequently, the possibility of developing a guidance system to effectively deliver the XW-8/REGULUS with pinpoint accuracy appeared remote. Consequently, on May 20, 1955, the Navy suspended activity in the program, together with work on the XW-11/REGULUS application.[69]

TX-10 External View

RS 3434/7

~~SECRET RESTRICTED DATA~~

TX-10 Weapon

The TX-10, a bomb that was never to achieve production, was to be an air-burst
version of the Mk 8. It was felt that, by deleting the requirement for target
penetration, the Mk 8 design could be considerably reduced in weight, and this
would allow the bomb to be carried by many additional types of aircraft. The
project was initially discussed in the May 6, 1948 meeting of the Sandia Research
and Development Board, which assigned priorities to a list of weapon design
projects proposed by the Armed Forces Special Weapons Project. The fourth item
was the development of a small gun-type air-burst device; this had a lower
priority than production of the Mk 4, development of the Mk 8 penetrating weapon,
or the task of reducing the size of the implosion bomb (which would result in the
Mk 5). [70]

Due to the effort required on more urgent programs, little work was immediately
undertaken on the gun-type air-burst bomb. Meanwhile, the Bureau of Ordnance
had started design of the Mk 8, and the Division of Military Application requested
the Bureau, in a letter dated January 21, 1949, to study the possibilities of
designing enough flexibility into the Mk 8 to permit its adaptation as an air-burst
weapon with weight as light as possible. [71]

No apparent action was taken at the time by the Bureau of Ordnance, and the
Military Liaison Committee subsequently commented, in a letter of April 22, 1949,
that little military need for such a device was foreseen for the immediate future,
and that only a very preliminary investigation of the project should be made. [72]
In reply, the Los Alamos Scientific Laboratory expressed surprise that the proposal
had not been accorded a more favorable reception. It was noted that the wartime
Little Boy was still being maintained on standby status, and that a lighter version of this same device (perhaps weighing about 2000 pounds as compared to the
8900-pound Little Boy) might be of value. [73]

However, the project lagged until the subject was again raised in a guided-missile
symposium at Sandia Base, March 7-8, 1950. The possibility of providing a lightweight gun device for a missile warhead was discussed, with Los Alamos suggesting
that such a warhead might weigh less than half that of the penetrating XW-8 Warhead,
which was estimated to weigh 3100 pounds. [47]

~~SECRET RESTRICTED DATA~~

Subsequently, the Division of Military Application proposed that a lightweight, air-burst, gun-type missile warhead be developed,[74] and this suggestion received the backing of the Military Liaison Committee July 6, 1950.[75] It was proposed that Army Ordnance, then involved with the Mk 9 Shell, be requested to assist in design and development.[76]

Meanwhile, the lightweight, air-burst, gun-type bomb project had not been entirely forgotten, and the Military Liaison Committee, in a letter dated August 9, 1950, stated that the Joint Chiefs of Staff had established a requirement for the development of air-burst bombs sufficiently light in weight and small in cross section to be carried by high-speed tactical airplanes of the Air Force and Navy. It was felt that these bombs could be based on either implosion- or gun-type nuclear devices, and formal requests were made for both types.[77]

The subject was discussed in the August 16, 1950 meeting of the Sandia Weapons Development Board, with the Board agreeing to assume cognizance of the project. Two problems were immediately apparent: The development of a flexible fuzing system capable of attacking various tactical targets, and a weapon resistant to temperatures as low as -100°F.[78]

Sandia had meanwhile made a study of a lightweight bomb design and reported to AEC-Sandia August 17, 1950, that this could be produced by mid-1952. It was suggested that North American Aviation, Inc., be assigned the task of developing and manufacturing the outer case, internal support structures, and parts of the carrying pylon. Sandia would develop a fuzing and firing system, conduct drop tests, provide test and handling equipment, and act as project coordinator.[79]

On the same date, the Division of Military Application forwarded military characteristics for the above bomb. These required that the bomb be capable of tactical use by fighter, light bombardment, and attack (dive bomber) aircraft. The primary requirement was for external carriage, with alternate internal carriage being desired.

(b)(1), (b)(3)

The Air Force desired nuclear safing, but the Navy was willing to forego this feature if the bomb could thereby be made available at an earlier date. It was requested that inflight monitoring or adjustments be as simple as possible, since the bomb would be carried on single-seat aircraft.

The bomb would have a maximum outer diameter of 14 inches and a weight of 1200 pounds. It should be capable of being effectively employed in high-altitude-delivery attacks to include horizontal, dive, toss or glide bombing. It would also be possible to release the bomb in a low-altitude shallow dive or level attack, with attendant safe withdrawal of the delivery aircraft. The bomb would be capable of release at subsonic or supersonic speeds, and would be able to operate successfully under a variety of climatic conditions, including icing and temperatures from -65°F to +165°F.[80]

On September 6, 1950 the Bureau of Ordnance replied to the Division of Military Application letter of January 21, 1949 that had requested design flexibility of the Mk 8 to permit use as a lightweight air-burst weapon. The Bureau noted that since the Mk 8 program was from 3 to 6 months ahead of schedule, personnel and facilities could now be diverted to work on the new design.[81]

The Division of Military Application replied October 3, 1950, noting that a lightweight air-burst bomb and a warhead had been considered to be nearly identical weapons. The warhead had originally been scheduled for use with the HERMES guided missile, but since the HERMES was now scheduled to carry an XW-7 implosion warhead, the need for a lightweight gun-type warhead had apparently vanished.[82] Since it was the policy of the Atomic Energy Commission to make full use of their own laboratories whenever possible, the development of a lightweight air-burst bomb would be handled by Sandia.[83]

The matter was discussed by the Sandia Weapons Development Board in a meeting October 18, 1950. The Board noted that it was becoming evident that implosion-type warheads could be designed to withstand missile flight environments of shock, acceleration, and vibration. As nuclear material was still scarce, and since implosion devices made more effective use of such material, a question was raised as to the economics of an air-burst gun-type warhead.

It had been previously estimated that the lightweight air-burst bomb could be produced earlier than the Mk 7, but Sandia representatives noted that the time scales of both weapons were roughly comparable. After considering the matter in some detail, the Board ruled that development of a lightweight, air-burst, gun-type bomb should continue, using the same nuclear components as the Mk 8.[84] Subsequently, Santa Fe Operations Office canceled the requirement for a lightweight air-burst warhead and reaffirmed the requirement for a lightweight air-burst and ground-burst gun-type bomb for both internal and external carriage.[85] North American Aviation, Inc., was requested to provide design and engineering models, and the air-burst bomb was officially designated as the TX-10.

Sandia proposed that the same aircraft being considered for TX-7 carriage be used to deliver the TX-10. These included the XA2D, XF10F, F84E and F84F for external carriage, and the B45 and XB51 for internal carriage. It was pointed out that the major advantages of the TX-10 included its small diameter and weight, and that these factors affected external carriage on fighter-bombers, but were not especially pertinent for internal carriage. Sandia proposed that the weapon diameter be between 14 and 18 inches, with the bomb having a minimum weight of 1750 pounds.

(b)(3)

Conferences between Sandia and the Bureau of Ordnance resulted in the issuance of a contract to the Bureau for development and proof testing of the TX-10 gun assembly. It was requested that automatic nuclear safing be provided if this could be accomplished by a reasonable expenditure of funds.[87] Santa Fe Operations Office formally transmitted this request to the Bureau of Ordnance November 28, 1950, noting that the TX-10 was now in full development, with the program directed toward ultimate production,[19] and the Bureau accepted the project in a letter of December 19, 1950.[20]

The TX-G or Gun Committee agreed to accept interlaboratory responsibility for the TX-10.[26] The program was subjected to an intensive review in a Committee meeting of December 14, 1950, with the TX-10 being compared with the TX-7, an implosion design that had been pushed rapidly and which was now scheduled to enter stockpile earlier than the TX-10. It was felt by some conferees that the basic need for the TX-10 was eliminated by the advent of the TX-7. This latter weapon was larger than the proposed diameter of the TX-10 (27 inches versus 17 inches), but there appeared to be a sufficient variety of airplanes that could carry the TX-7.

(b)(1), (b)(3)

The problem was referred to the Sandia Weapons Development Board and discussed in a meeting December 20, 1950, with the Board being furnished copies of Sandia Report SC-1684(TR), A Critical Comparison Between the TX-7 and TX-10 Programs. This report noted that design was in work on a follow-on (and smaller) implosion device for the TX-7 (to be called the TX-12). The TX-12 would be less costly from the nuclear standpoint, would offer greater chances of increasing nuclear efficiency, and could be developed in about the same time scales. It was pointed out that work on the TX-10 would subtract effort from the TX-12, and that tactical use of the TX-10 (if manufactured in large numbers) would require major realignment of component production.

The Board noted that the TX-10 diameter would probably be smaller than the TX-7 or TX-12, but stated that further reductions in implosion-weapon diameter could be expected, as much nuclear design effort was currently being placed on implosion design improvements. After extensive discussion, the Board recommended that the TX-10 development be dropped in favor of the TX-12.[89]

The Division of Military Application wrote to Santa Fe Operations Office January 3, 1951, making reference to the above meeting. There were hopes that an interim TX-10 could be made available earlier than the TX-12, and it was suggested that the requirement for nuclear safing be eliminated and an external shape suitable for subsonic (but not necessarily supersonic) carriage be provided.[90]

This letter was discussed in a special meeting of the TX-G Committee January 16, 1951. Los Alamos stated that they could not undertake improvements to gun-type nuclear designs for another 6 months, and recommended that the Mk 8 nuclear design be used without change. This proposal was adopted by the Committee. The Bureau of Ordnance proposed a "quick and dirty" TX-10 design without nuclear safing and a minor lightening of the internal gun barrel. It was felt that the Bureau of Ordnance could produce a prototype in about 6 months. Sandia stated that 2-1/2 years had been allocated for fuzing development, but that this time could be shortened by 1 year if the project were assigned high priority. [91]

The above information was furnished to the Division of Military Application, which referred the problem to the Military Liaison Committee February 12, 1951. It was noted that acceleration of engineering work could be justified only if there were a production requirement based on operational use of the TX-10 before the stockpile date of the TX-7, and that such requirement did not presently exist. The Division of Military Application pointed out that adequate development of gun-type weapons was assured by the TX-9 and TX-11 programs, both of which required nuclear safing, and recommended that the TX-10 program be canceled. [92]

The above suggestion was turned down by the Military Liaison Committee, which requested that the TX-10 development continue, but on the basis of noninterference with other programs. It was suggested that this time extension would allow design of nuclear safing and provide for carriage on supersonic aircraft. [93]

Sandia subsequently started study of a TX-10 Fuze. An air-burst weapon would logically require a radar fuze, but requirements for low-level release meant that the bomb would be almost horizontal at burst altitude and would have difficulty ranging off the target, since the antennas were pointing straight ahead. Timer fuzing systems were thus also included in the study. [94]

The Armed Forces Special Weapons Project suggested that the extension of time might allow development of an approximately zero-height-of-burst design, together with safe-separation devices for protection of the carrying aircraft, and improved antijamming versions of the radar fuze. The desire for minimum size and weight was re-emphasized, and figures of 14-inch diameter and 1200-pound weight were noted. [95]

RS 3434/7

The design status of the TX-10 was reviewed in the April 10, 1951 meeting of the Sandia Weapons Development Board. The bomb would be at least 17 inches in diameter and 2000 pounds in weight.

(b)(3), (b)(1)

The Board noted that the diameter and weight of the TX-10 exceeded the military characteristics, and that major reductions in these items could not be expected until the nuclear gun design was revised by Los Alamos.

(b)(3)

The project thus reverted to fundamental study of the problems of providing low burst heights, miniaturization, supersonic aerodynamics, and nuclear design improvements. Subsequently, the Military Liaison Committee canceled the TX-10 Bomb program May 7, 1952, noting that the Joint Chiefs of Staff had stated that a military requirement for the weapon no longer existed.

(b)(3)

-35-

RS 3434/7

(b)(1), (b)(3)

Mk 91 Mod 0 Bomb Cross Section

Mk 11 Weapon

The Mk 11 Bomb, a gun-type penetrating weapon to be externally carried on high-speed aircraft, had its early beginnings when the gun-type device was considered for guided-missile application in March 1950. In this usage nuclear safing would be required to protect the missile launching site, and it would be necessary for the warhead to survive high impact velocities.[47]

Subsequently, the Division of Military Application expressed interest in a gun-type bomb that could be nuclearly safed and externally carried on high-speed aircraft.[99] The external shape of the Mk 8 did not lend itself to such carriage (due chiefly to its blunt nose), and it was felt that any modification of the nose shape would be complicated by the existence of the nose fuze. A nose redesign would require a lengthy effort, and it was suggested that a development program be authorized for a Mk II Elsie for such usage.[100]

The Military Liaison Committee released a set of desired military and technical characteristics for impact, delayed-action atomic bombs April 17, 1950. These characteristics described a bomb which could be nuclearly safed during aircraft carriage and that would be suitable for release at speeds up to Mach 1.2.[54] Subsequently, July 31, 1950, the Division of Military Application requested the Bureau of Ordnance to design a Mk 8-type weapon meeting these characteristics, and offered Sandia assistance in the task of fitting the design to appropriate carrying aircraft.[101] This proposal was accepted by the Bureau of Ordnance,[102] and nomenclature of TX-11 was assigned to the project November 29, 1950.[103]

There were three main gun-weapon problems being studied at this time: The ballistics problem relating to external carriage and release at high speeds; the nuclear safing problem, which concerned missiles as well as bombs; and the problem of increasing the resistance of the weapon to impacts on hard targets, such as reinforced concrete, rock and armor plate.

The Naval Ordnance Laboratory started to design the TX-11 fuzing system. It was felt that feasibility and preliminary design studies to establish tentative characteristics could be completed by January 1, 1952; and that detailed design and manufacture of prototype fuzes could be finished by October 1, 1953. The fuze would have to function reliably when externally carried at speeds up to Mach 1.2, altitudes up to 50,000 feet, and within a temperature range of -100°F to +125°F. The weapon would survive impacts on water, 4-inch steel plate, and ricochets off hard rock.[104]

The TX-11 project was given close examination in the May 31, 1951 meeting of the TX-G Steering Committee. Studies had shown that a streamlined bomb would have a terminal velocity of about 2000 feet per second, higher than originally predicted, and it was suggested that the bomb shape be given increased drag to reduce this velocity.

After considerable discussion, it was decided that two design approaches would be pursued. The first, called Program A, would provide a weapon to survive impacts with reinforced concrete at speeds of 1500 feet per second, but not survive impacts at 2500 feet per second. An optional drag mechanism would be provided to retard weapon speed. Program B would develop a bomb with high survival probability against hard targets at velocities of 2700 feet per second (Mach 2.5) or higher, and this design could be used in a missile warhead.[105] The TX-G Committee, in a meeting June 23, 1951, felt that emphasis should be placed on Program A, and that work on Program B should be delayed pending results of impact studies being pursued by the Bureau of Ordnance.[106]

On July 24, 1951, Sandia suggested that the Bureau of Ordnance develop and proof-test the necessary adaptations to the TX-11 Bomb to allow use as a warhead with the REGULUS, RIGEL and HERMES missiles. This program was felt to be the initial step toward providing impact-resistant warheads for missiles with speeds as high as Mach 4.5, and was firmed up in mid-August 1951.[107]

The desired military characteristics for the TX-11 were issued in August 1951[108] and discussed in a meeting of the Sandia Weapons Development Board January 16, 1952. These characteristics noted that the purpose of the bomb was to attack targets susceptible to destruction by subsurface atomic burst. The weight of the bomb would not exceed 3600 pounds and the maximum diameter would be 14 inches, exclusive of fins. The bomb would be used in high- and low-altitude attacks, including horizontal, toss, glide and dive bombing. It would be capable of carriage and release at speeds up to Mach 1.4 and altitudes of 50,000 feet. It would be able to function satisfactorily after impacts on water, soil, reinforced concrete, and--to the extent practicable--harder targets.

The Board noted that the characteristics required external carriage at both subsonic and supersonic speeds, but a shape designed for one of these velocities would not be optimum for the other. It was felt that the design should be based on the assumption that the least drag during the major portion of the flight was desirable. Inasmuch as jet fighters en route to a target cruised at subsonic speeds, the bomb shape should be designed to meet this requirement.

The desire that the weapon be capable of penetration into hard rock was of concern. It was difficult to suitably define "hard rock," and there was felt to be a low incidence of this type of terrain near any probable targets. The scheduled design-release date was established as October 1953, with the bomb to enter stockpile in January 1955.[34]

The Bureau of Ordnance had been conducting tests of a soft-steel nose cap which, it was hoped, would crush and absorb the shock of weapon impact. These tests were not encouraging, and it was eventually decided to provide a Fiberglas nose cap. When the bomb was to be carried in an internal bomb bay, this nose cap could be removed.

Wind-tunnel tests had meanwhile narrowed the choice of weapon length to two possibilities; 146 and 169 inches. The Bureau of Ordnance recommended that the shorter figure be selected: It caused less drag at subsonic speed, it was compatible with all aircraft being considered for carriage of the bomb, and it could be carried internally in all aircraft except the B-50 without removing the nose cap.[109]

Full-scale drops at Inyokern produced excellent results.

(b)(1), (b)(3)

No detonation of the high explosive occurred during any of the impacts. Tests of 6-1/4-inch-diameter scale models against reinforced concrete 10 feet thick demonstrated that impact velocities between 2000 and 2200 feet per second could be

RS 3434/7

absorbed.[110]   As a result of these tests, the length of the TX-11 was frozen at 146 inches on June 30, 1952, and the fin size was established at two bomb diameters, or 28 inches.[111]

Meanwhile, work had been undertaken on the design of a nuclear safing system,

(b)(3)

Meanwhile, some effort had been applied to gun-type missile warhead design.[114] Bureau of Ordnance studies noted that a maximum impact velocity of Mach 2.5 should be considered.[115] The Division of Military Application notified the Military Liaison Committee April 1, 1952, that the XW-8 Warhead could survive the relatively low impact velocity of the REGULUS, and that this missile-warhead combination should be released for early production. It was noted that other missiles, such as the HERMES, REDSTONE, RIGEL AND TRITON, had impact velocities that substantially exceeded even the impact resistance of the TX-11. It appeared, therefore, that an extensive development program would be required,[60] and the XW-11 Warhead was subsequently dropped.[116]

Meanwhile, the design-release date of the TX-11 had been slipping as a result of work on the safing problem, and in early 1953 a new release date of April 1, 1954 was established.[117] This delay was approved by the Division of Military Application in a letter April 21, 1953, which noted that the Navy would soon assume production responsibilities for the bomb.[118] This transfer was effected July 1, 1953, and guidance of development activities placed in the hands of the Aspen Committee, which contained members from Los Alamos, Bureau of Ordnance, the Armed Forces Special Weapons Project, and Sandia.[119]

Initially, it had been proposed to assign the nomenclature of Mk 11 when the TX-11 entered production. However, this title had previously been applied to a Navy practice bomb, and the production version of the TX-11 was named the Mk 91 Mod 0 in mid-1954.[120] The design-release date was April 1, 1955; first production units became available January 1, 1956; and the Mk 91 entered stockpile July 1, 1956. Mk 8 Bombs were retired on a one-for-one basis after the Mk 91's entered stockpile.

The following Air Force aircraft were specified as carriers: B-36D, B-36F, B-45A, B-47B, B-52A, B-57A, B-66A, F-84F, F-84G, F-84X, F-100A and F-101A. Navy carriers included the AD5, AD5N, AD6, AJ1, AJ2, A2D1, A3D1, F2H3, F2H4, F3H1, F7U3 and F10F1.

The Mk 91 Bomb was 14 inches in diameter, 28 inches across the fins, 146 inches long, and its weight was 3350 pounds. The fuzing system contained two Mk 250 time-delay fuzes, each capable of independently igniting the internal gun propellant charge.

RS 3434/7

The fuzes were mechanically armed and were of a pyrotechnic design similar to those used in the Mk 8.

(b)(1), (b)(3)

Glossary of Terms

<u>Ad Hoc Working Group</u> -- A group established by the Guided Missiles Committee to oversee the design of one particular missile-warhead installation.

<u>Armed Forces Special Weapons Project</u> -- An interdepartmental agency formed to handle military functions related to atomic weapons.

(b)(1), (b)(3)

<u>Contact Fuze</u> -- A fuze that detonates the weapon by contact with the ground or target.

<u>Crossroads</u> -- Full-scale tests of Mk III Bombs, held at the Pacific Proving Grounds. The Bikini Baker shot was held July 25, 1946. Much effects data were gained, and the shot was so destructive that a scheduled deep underwater burst was canceled.

<u>Division of Military Application</u> -- An AEC office that functions as liaison between the Military and weapons designers and producers.

<u>Drag</u> -- Resistance created by the passage of a shape through the air.

<u>Field Command</u> -- The local office of the Armed Forces Special Weapons Project, located on Sandia Base, Albuquerque, New Mexico.

RS 3434/7

Frangible -- Breakable.

Fuze -- A combination of the arming and firing devices of a weapon.

g -- Force equal to one unit gravity.

General Advisory Committee -- A group established by the Atomic Energy Act to provide policy direction for the Atomic Energy Commission.

Groves, Major General Leslie R. -- Wartime head of the Manhattan Engineer District.

Guided Missiles Committee -- A committee established by the Sandia Research and Development Board to function as liaison between the Board and the various committees for each missile-warhead combination.

Gun Committee -- A joint committee of Los Alamos and Sandia members, established to guide the development of all gun-type weapons.

Gun-Type Design -- An atomic weapon based on the principle that a supercritical mass of nuclear material can be created by bringing together two subcritical masses of such material. In practice, this is accomplished by placing one of the subcritical masses at the end of a gun barrel and shooting the other subcritical mass into it.

Implosion -- The effect created when a sphere of high explosive is detonated on its exterior surface. The force of the shock wave is directed largely toward the center of the sphere.

Initiator -- A source of neutrons.

Inyokern -- A Naval Ordnance Test Station located in the Mojave Desert at Inyokern, California.

Joint Chiefs of Staff -- An Army-Navy-Air Force group to determine policy and to develop joint strategic objectives of the Armed Forces.

Joint Research and Development Board -- A Board established in mid-1946 as a postwar replacement for the Office of Scientific Research and Development. Its purpose was to suggest lines of research and development on military weapons and equipment.

Kiloton -- A means of measuring the yield of an atomic device by comparing its output with the effect of an explosion of TNT. A 1-kiloton yield is equivalent to the detonation effect of 1000 tons of high explosive.

Little Boy -- Code name for the gun-type weapon dropped on Hiroshima, Japan, August 6, 1945, during World War II. Originally called the Thin Man in reference to its long thin shape. The Thin Man was to use plutonium-239 as its nuclear material. Early samples of this isotope revealed that it contained small amounts of plutonium-240 which had a high preinitiation rate. A decision was then made to use uranium-235, allowing the length of the weapon to be radically reduced (due to the lower speed of assembly of the critical material). This change in outer shape was given the code name of Little Boy.

Los Alamos Scientific Laboratory -- A nuclear design organization located at Los Alamos, New Mexico. Called the Los Alamos Laboratory during World War II.

Mach -- A measure of speed. Mach 1.0 is the speed of sound, or 738 miles per hour at sea level.

Manhattan Engineer District -- A District of the Army Engineers established in August 1942 to provide the facilities that would be needed for design and construction of the atomic bomb.

Military Characteristics -- The attributes of a weapon that are desired by the Military.

Military Liaison Committee -- A Department of Defense committee established by the Atomic Energy Act to advise and consult with the AEC on all matters relating to military applications of atomic energy.

Naval Ordnance Laboratory -- A portion of the Bureau of Ordnance devoted to design and test of Naval ordnance.

Neutron -- An uncharged particle of slightly greater mass than the proton.

Operation Crossroads -- See Crossroads.

Pitch -- Motion of the bomb as it falls through the air, such that the nose and tail alternately rise and fall.

Proton -- The nucleus of the atom of the light isotope of hydrogen. It has a unit positive charge of electricity.

Prototype -- An early weapon type, generally hand-produced before a production run.

Pylon -- A strut to hold bomb in position below an airplane wing.

Pyrotechnic Fuze -- A fuze that operates by burning or detonation of a small charge of explosive.

Radar -- Named for **Ra**dio **D**etecting **an**d **R**anging. Radars emit a pulse of high-frequency energy and measure the time lapse from that transmission to receipt of a reflected electrical "echo" from an object. This time measurement determines the distance of the object from the transmitting antenna of the radar.

Ricochet -- A glancing rebound of a missile when it strikes a target.

Safing -- Putting a weapon in condition such that it cannot fire.

Salton Sea Test Base -- Located on the site of a Naval Auxiliary Air Station on the shores of Salton Sea, California. One of the early sites for ballistic tests of atomic bombs.

Sandia Research and Development Board -- A joint Sandia-Military board formed March 2, 1948, at Sandia Base to provide local guidance on weapons design.

Sandia Weapons Development Board -- Change of name for the Sandia Research and Development Board, effective May 24, 1950.

Santa Fe Operations Office -- The local office of the Atomic Energy Commission (AEC) concerned with Sandia operations.

Special Weapons Development Board -- Change of name for the Sandia Weapons Development Board, effective May 14, 1952.

Subsonic -- Any speed below that of Mach 1.0, which is the speed of sound, or 738 miles per hour at sea level.

Supercriticality -- The state of being ready to fission.

Supersonic -- Any speed exceeding that of Mach 1.0, which is the speed of sound, or 738 miles per hour at sea level.

Tamper -- A hollow shell of relatively dense material *normally part of the ___* that surrounds the nuclear charge and acts as a reflector for neutrons that might otherwise escape from the nuclear reaction.

Terraballistics -- Ballistics of a weapon after it penetrates the terrain.

Toss Bombing -- A flight technique for delivering bombs in which the aircraft releases the weapon while climbing.

TX Committee -- A joint committee of Los Alamos and Sandia members, established to guide the development of implosion-type weapons. Initially called the TX-N Committee.

TX-G Steering Committee -- A joint committee of Los Alamos and Sandia members, established to guide the development of gun-type weapons.

Uranium-235 -- A radioactive element, an isotope of uranium-238.

Uranium-238 -- A radioactive element, atomic number 92. Natural uranium contains about 99.3-percent of uranium-238; the rest is uranium-235.

Z Division -- A division of the Los Alamos Scientific Laboratory, elements of which moved to Sandia Base and became the nucleus of Sandia Laboratory and Corporation.

UNCLASSIFIED

UNCLASSIFIED

RS 3434/7

References

1.

2.

(b)(3)

3.

4. SRD Ltr, Division of Military Application to Santa Fe Operations Office, dtd 1/6/48, subject, Penetrating Weapon. AEC Files, Folder 471.6.

5. SRD Ltr, Committee on Atomic Energy to Research and Development Board, dtd 10/20/47, subject, Penetration-Type Atomic Weapons. AEC Files, Folder 471.6.

6. SRD Ltr, Los Alamos Scientific Laboratory to Santa Fe Operations Office, dtd 1/15/48, subject, Penetration Weapon. AEC Files, Folder 471.6.

7. SRD Ltr, U. S. Atomic Energy Commission to Military Liaison Committee, dtd 2/26/48. AEC Files, Folder 471.6.

8. SRD Ltr, Military Liaison Committee to U. S. Atomic Energy Commission, dtd 4/9/48. AEC Files, Folder 471.6.

9. SRD Ltr, U. S. Atomic Energy Commission to Bureau of Ordnance, dtd 4/27/48. AEC Files, Folder 471.6.

10. SRD Ltr, Bureau of Ordnance to Naval Proving Grounds, Dahlgren, Virginia, dtd 7/15/48, subject, Project Elsie - Assignment of Tasks. AEC Files, MRA, Mk 8-10-11, 6/48-8/49.

11. SRD Ltr, Bureau of Ordnance to U. S. Atomic Energy Commission, dtd 9/3/48, subject, Subsurface Weapon - Status of Development - Preliminary Outline of Proposed Program. AEC Files, MRA, Mk 8-10-11, 6/48-8/49.

UNCLASSIFIED

RS 3434/7

12. SRD Ltr, Los Alamos Scientific Laboratory to Bureau of Aeronautics, dtd 11/5/48, subject, Subsurface Weapon Project (Project Elsie) Conference at Los Alamos, October 25 and 26, 1948. AEC Files, MRA, Mk 8-10-11, 6/48-8/49.

13. SRD Ltr, Division of Military Application to Sandia Corporation, dtd 11/18/49, subject, Sandia Participation in Project Elsie. SC Archives, microfilm reel MF-SF-SC-45.

14. SRD Ltr, Sandia Corporation to Division of Military Application, dtd 2/1/50, subject, Sandia Participation in Elsie Project. SC Archives, microfilm reel MF-SF-SC-45.

15. CRD Ltr, RS 1212/4075, H. W. Russ, 1212, to R. A. Bice, 1210, dtd 4/17/50, subject, Tentative Program of Ordnance Division C in Connection with Project Elsie. SC Archives, microfilm reel MF-SF-SC-45.

16. SRD Ltr, RS 1/45, Sandia Corporation to Division of Military Application, dtd 7/28/50, subject, Procurement of Elsie Components. SC Archives, microfilm reel MF-SF-SC-45.

17. SRD Ltr, AEC-Sandia to Sandia Corporation, dtd 8/30/50, subject, Elsie War Reserve Program. SC Archives, microfilm reel MF-SF-SC-29.

18. SRD Report, Los Alamos Scientific Laboratory to Distribution, dtd 9/2/50, subject, Notes of 1 September Meeting Regarding TX-8 Handling Problems. SC Archives, microfilm reel MF-SF-SC-29.

19. SRD Ltr, Santa Fe Operations Office to Bureau of Ordnance, dtd 11/28/50, subject, Proposed Participation of Bureau of Ordnance in Gun-Type Weapon Development Programs. SC Archives, microfilm reel MF-SF-SC-45.

20. SRD Ltr, Bureau of Ordnance to Santa Fe Operations Office, dtd 12/19/50, subject, Proposed Participation of Bureau of Ordnance in Gun-Type Weapons Development Programs. SC Archives, microfilm reel MF-SF-SC-45.

RS 3434/7

21. SRD Ltr, Division of Military Application to Military Liaison Committee, dtd 10/3/50, subject, External Suspension for Elsie Weapons. AEC Files, MRA, Mk 8-10-11, 7/50-12/50.

22.

(b)(3)

23. SRD Ltr, Los Alamos Scientific Laboratory to Santa Fe Operations Office, dtd 9/27/49, subject, Desired Military and Technical Characteristics of Penetrating-Type Atomic Weapons. AEC Files, MRA-9, 7/1/49-6/30/50.

24.

(b)(3)

25. SRD Minutes, RS 3466/67993, Sandia Weapons Development Board to Distribution, dtd 11/22/50, subject, Minutes of 46th Meeting. SC Archives, Transfer No. 48217.

26. SRD Minutes, RS 3466/60614, Gun Committee to Distribution, dtd 12/8/50, subject, Minutes of 1st Meeting. SC Reports Library.

27.

(b)(3)

28.

29. SRD Report, Sandia Corporation to Distribution, dtd 7/1/51, subject, SC1936(TR), An Evaluation of the TX-8' (Externally-Carried Mk 8 Weapon). SC Reports Library.

30. SRD Ltr, RS 1/148, Sandia Corporation to Santa Fe Operations Office, dtd 7/31/51, subject, TX-8 Prime Program Summary and Recommendations. SC Archives, Transfer No. 29888.

31. SRD Minutes, RS 3466/61004, Sandia Weapons Development Board to Distribution, dtd 8/8/51, subject, Minutes of the 54th Meeting. SC Archives, Transfer No. 48217.

32. SRD Ltr, Division of Military Application to Santa Fe Operations Office, dtd 9/10/51, subject, TX-8 Prime Program. SC Archives, microfilm reel MF-SF-SC-1437.

33. SRD Ltr, RS 1200/432, Sandia Corporation to Field Command, dtd 10/29/51, subject, Externally Carried TX-8 Weapon. SC Archives, microfilm reel MF-SF-SC-1437.

34. SRD Minutes, RS 3466/60958, Sandia Weapons Development Board to Distribution, dtd 1/16/52, subject, Minutes of 59th Meeting. SC Archives, Transfer No. 48217.

35. SRD Ltr, RS 1/222, Sandia Corporation to AEC-Sandia, dtd 2/5/52, subject, Mark 8 Modification. SC Archives, Transfer No. 29880.

36.

37.   (b)(3)

38. SRD Minutes, RS 3466/62057, Sandia Weapons Development Board to Distribution, dtd 4/16/52, subject, Minutes of 61st Meeting. SC Archives, Transfer No. 48217.

39.

                                            (b)(3)

40. SRD Ltr, Military Liaison Committee to Division of Military Application, dtd 10/20/52, subject, Production of the Mk 8 Mod 0 Bomb. AEC Files, MBA, Mk 8-10-11, 10/52-11/53.

41. SRD Ltr, RS 1000/1041, Sandia Corporation to Bureau of Ordnance, dtd 7/18/52, subject, Mk 8 Characteristics, Request for Study. AEC Files, MBA, Mk 8-10-11, 7/52-9/52.

42. SRD Ltr, Division of Military Application to Military Liaison Committee, dtd 5/14/53, subject, Final Approval - Mk 8 Bomb with Mk 8 Mod 1 Fuze (Formerly TX-8-X2). AEC Files, MBA, Mk 8-10-11, 4/53-6/53.

43. SRD Ltr, RS 3466/141920, Division of Military Application to Sandia Corporation, dtd 3/12/53, subject, Temperature and Operational Limitations of the Mk 8 Mod 0 Bomb. SC Archives, Transfer No. 29745.

44. CRD Ltr, RS 1000/1697, Sandia Corporation to Santa Fe Operations Office, dtd 12/17/54, subject, Nomenclature Change to Mk 8 Bomb, TX-8-X3 Program. SC Archives, Transfer No. 29745.

45. SRD Ltr, RS 1/701, Sandia Corporation to Santa Fe Operations Office, dtd 3/31/55, subject, Transfer of Mk 8 Responsibilities. SC Archives, Transfer No. 29745.

46. SRD Ltr, RS 3466/139263, Santa Fe Operations Office to Sandia Corporation, dtd 4/27/55, subject, Transfer of Mk 8 Responsibilities. SC Archives, Transfer No. 32715-7, Folders 8 and 9.

47. SRD Ltr, Los Alamos Scientific Laboratory to Distribution, dtd 3/9/50, subject, Rough Draft of Notes for Meeting at Sandia on Guided Missiles, By A. R. Sayer, W-1. SC Archives, microfilm reel MF-SF-SC-1459.

48. SRD Ltr, Santa Fe Operations Office to Sandia Corporation and Los Alamos Scientific Laboratory, dtd 9/13/50, subject, Gun-Type Weapon Program, Addendum No. 1, 46th Meeting, Sandia Weapons Development Board. SC Archives, Transfer No. 48217.

49. SRD Ltr, Bureau of Ordnance to U. S. Atomic Energy Commission, dtd 10/24/50, subject, Atomic Warheads for Guided Missiles. AEC Files, Guided Missiles.

50. SRD Ltr, Division of Military Application to Bureau of Ordnance, dtd 11/1/50. SC Archives, microfilm reel MF-SF-SC-1447.

51. SRD Ltr, RS 1/89, Sandia Corporation to AEC-Sandia, dtd 12/20/50, subject, Gun-Type Atomic Warheads for Guided Missiles. AEC Files, MRA-5, 7/50-6/51.

52. SRD Ltr, AEC-Sandia to Sandia Corporation, dtd 1/23/51, subject, Atomic Warheads for Guided Missiles. SC Archives, microfilm reel MF-SF-SC-138.

53. SRD Ltr, Sandia Corporation to Field Command, dtd 1/23/51, subject, Sandia Corporation Preliminary Comments on Military Characteristics for Atomic Warheads for REGULUS. AEC Files, Guided Missiles.

54. SRD Ltr, Santa Fe Operations Office to Sandia Corporation and Los Alamos Scientific Laboratory, dtd 2/14/51, subject, Gun-Type Weapon Program. SC Archives, microfilm reel MF-SF-SC-47.

55. SRD Ltr, RS 1/104, Sandia Corporation to AEC-Sandia, dtd 2/19/51, subject, TX-8 (Elsie) Warhead for the REGULUS Missile. AEC Files, MRA-5, REGULUS, Volume I.

56. SRD Minutes, RS 3466/60796, Sandia Weapons Development Board to Distribution, dtd 4/10/51, subject, Minutes of the 50th Meeting. SC Archives, Transfer No. 48217.

57. SRD Ltr, Sandia Corporation to TX-G Committee, dtd 12/51, subject, Status of XW-8/REGULUS. AEC Files, Guided Missiles.

58. SRD Ltr, Field Command to Distribution, dtd 1/18/52, subject, Relative Priorities for XW-5 and XW-8 Warheads for REGULUS Missile. AEC Files, Guided Missiles.

59. SRD Ltr, Bureau of Ordnance to Santa Fe Operations Office, dtd 2/26/52, subject, Adaptation of Gun-Type Atomic Warheads to Guided Missiles. SC Archives, microfilm reel MF-SF-SC-103.

60. SRD Ltr, RS 3421-4/2082, Division of Military Application to Military Liaison Committee, dtd 4/1/52, subject, Penetration Atomic Warheads for Guided Missiles. SC Archives, microfilm reel MF-SF-SC-103.

61. SRD Minutes, XW-5/REGULUS Ad Hoc Working Group to Distribution, dtd 6/27/52, subject, Minutes of 5th Meeting. AEC Files, MRA-5.

62. SRD Minutes, XW-5/REGULUS Ad Hoc Working Group to Distribution, dtd 7/29/52, subject, Minutes of 6th Meeting. AEC Files, MRA-5.

63. SRD Ltr, Guided Missiles Committee to Special Weapons Development Board, dtd 8/15/52. AEC Files, Guided Missiles.

64. SRD Ltr, Field Command to Sandia Corporation, dtd 8/21/52, subject, Proposed Military Characteristics for the XW-8/REGULUS, Transmittal of. AEC Files, MRA-5, REGULUS, Volume I.

65. SRD Ltr, Division of Military Application to Santa Fe Operations Office, dtd 10/21/52, subject, Penetration Atomic Warhead for Guided Missiles. AEC Files, MRA-5, 9/52-10/52.

66. SRD Ltr, Santa Fe Operations Office to AEC-Sandia, dtd 6/29/53, subject, XW-8/REGULUS. AEC Files, MRA-5, REGULUS, Volume III.

67. SRD Ltr, Military Liaison Committee to U. S. Atomic Energy Commission, dtd 11/25/53, subject, XW-8/REGULUS Warhead Installation Development Program. AEC Files, MRA-5, 11/53-1/54.

68. SRD Minutes, RS 3466/81765, Special Weapons Development Board to Distribution, dtd 12/1/54, subject, Minutes of 88th Meeting, Part I. SC Archives, Transfer No. 48217.

69. SRD Ltr, Chief of Naval Operations to Distribution, dtd 5/20/55, subject, Penetrating Atomic Warhead Program for the REGULUS I Guided Missile; Termination of. AEC Files, MRA-5, REGULUS, 1/55.

70. SRD Minutes, RS 3466/60124, Sandia Research and Development Board to Distribution, dtd 5/6/48, subject, Minutes of 6th Meeting. SC Archives, Transfer No. 48217.

71. SRD Ltr, Division of Military Application to Bureau of Ordnance, dtd 1/21/49, subject, Project Elsie. AEC Files, MRA, Mk 8-10-11, 6/48-8/49.

72. SRD Ltr, Military Liaison Committee to Division of Military Application, dtd 4/22/49, subject, Additional Specification of Objective in Subsurface Weapon Development. AEC Files, MRA, Mk 8-10-11, 6/48-8/49.

73. SRD Ltr, Los Alamos Scientific Laboratory to Division of Military Application, dtd 5/19/49, subject, Elsie Specifications. AEC Files, MRA, Mk 8-10-11, 6/48-8/49.

74. SRD Ltr, Division of Military Application to Santa Fe Operations Office, dtd 3/30/50, subject, Weapon Development Program. AEC Files, MRA-9, 7/49-6/50.

75. SRD Ltr, RS 3421-4/2157, Military Liaison Committee to Division of Military Application, dtd 7/6/50, subject, Guided Missiles with Atomic Warheads. SC Archives, microfilm reel MF-SF-SC-1459.

76. SRD Ltr, RS 3421-4/2156, Division of Military Application to Santa Fe Operations Office, dtd 7/27/50, subject, Guided Missiles with Atomic Warheads. SC Archives, microfilm reel MF-SF-SC-1459.

77. SRD Ltr, RS 3421-4/2639, Military Liaison Committee to Division of Military Application, dtd 8/9/50, subject, Lightweight Airburst Atomic Bomb. SC Archives, microfilm reel MF-SF-SC-1440.

78. SRD Minutes, RS 3466/67992, Sandia Weapons Development Board to Distribution, dtd 8/lo/50, subject, Minutes of 43rd Meeting. SC Archives, Transfer No. 48217.

UNCLASSIFI

79. SRD Ltr, RS 1/57, Sandia Corporation to AEC-Sandia, dtd 8/17/50, subject,
Plans for Development of an Air Burst Elsie Weapon. AEC Files, MRA, 9-1,
TX-10, Volume I.

80. SRD Ltr, Division of Military Application to Santa Fe Operations Office,
dtd 8/17/50, subject, Lightweight Air Burst Bomb. AEC Files, MRA, Mk 7,
6/50-6/51.

81. SRD Ltr, Bureau of Ordnance to U. S. Atomic Energy Commission, dtd 9/6/50,
subject, Lightweight Airburst Gun-Type Bomb. AEC Files, MRA, 9-1, TX-10,
Volume I.

82. SRD Ltr, Division of Military Application to Santa Fe Operations Office, dtd
10/3/50, subject, Allocation of Development and Production Responsibilities to
Contractors, with Particular Reference to Gun-Type Weapon Program. AEC Files,
MRA, Mk 8-10-11, 7/50-12/50.

83. SRD Ltr, Division of Military Application to Bureau of Ordnance, dtd 10/3/50.
AEC Files, MRA, 9-1, TX-10, Volume I.

84. SRD Minutes, RS 3466/90268, Sandia Weapons Development Board to Distribution,
dtd 10/18/50, subject, Minutes of 45th Meeting. SC Archives, Transfer No.
48217.

85. SRD Ltr, Santa Fe Operations Office to Los Alamos Scientific Laboratory and
Sandia Corporation, dtd 10/23/50, subject, Gun-Type Weapon Program. AEC Files,
MRA, 9-1, TX-10, Volume I.

86.

(b)(3)

87. SRD Ltr, Sandia Corporation to Santa Fe Operations Office, dtd 11/13/50, subject,
Proposed Contract Agreements for TX-8 External and TX-10. SC Archives, microfilm
reel MF-SF-SC-1439.

UNCLASSIFIED

88.

(b)(3)

89. SRD Minutes, RS 3466/60396, Sandia Weapons Development Board to Distribution, dtd 12/20/50, subject, Minutes of 47th Meeting. SC Archives, Transfer No. 48217.

90. SRD Ltr, Division of Military Application to Santa Fe Operations Office, dtd 1/3/51, subject, Airburst Elsie. AEC Files, MRA-9, Elsie, Mk 8, 1/51-3/51.

91. SRD Minutes, RS 3466/60394, TX-G Committee to Distribution, dtd 1/16/51, subject, Minutes of 4th Meeting. SC Reports Files.

92. SRD Ltr, Division of Military Application to Military Liaison Committee, dtd 2/12/51, subject, TX-10 Development. AEC Files, MRA-9, Elsie, Mk 8, 1/51-3/51.

93. SRD Ltr, Division of Military Application to Santa Fe Operations Office, dtd 3/7/51, subject, TX-10 Development. AEC Files, MRA-9, Elsie, Mk 8, 1/51-3/51.

94. SRD Minutes, RS 3421-4/2307, Advisory Committee on Fuzing to Distribution, dtd 3/9/51, subject, Minutes of Meeting. SC Archives, microfilm reel MF-SF-SC-85.

95. SRD Ltr, RS 3421-4/2671, Field Command to Sandia Corporation, dtd 4/5/51, subject, TX-10 Weapon Development. SC Archives, microfilm reel MF-SF-SC-29.

96.

97.

(b)(3)

98.

UNCLASSIFIED

99. SRD Ltr, AEC-Sandia to Sandia Corporation, dtd 8/1/50, subject, External Suspension of Elsie Weapon. SC Archives, microfilm reel MF-SF-SC-29.

100. SRD Ltr, RS 1/47, Sandia Corporation to Division of Military Application, dtd 8/1/50, subject, Elsie as an External Store. SC Archives, microfilm reel MF-SF-SC-47.

101. SRD Ltr, Division of Military Application to Bureau of Ordnance, dtd 7/31/50, subject, External Suspension of Elsie Weapon. AEC Files, MRA, Mk 8-10-11, 7/50-12/50.

102. SRD Ltr, Santa Fe Operations Office to Bureau of Ordnance, dtd 3/8/51, subject, BuOrd Participation in the TX-11 Program. AEC Files, MRA-9, Elsie, 1/51-3/51.

103. SRD Ltr, Santa Fe Operations Office to AEC-Sandia, dtd 11/29/50, subject, Nomenclature for Weapons under Development. AEC Files, MRA-9, Nomenclature, 7/1/50.

104. SRD Ltr, RS 3421-4/2550, Bureau of Ordnance to Naval Ordnance Laboratory, dtd 4/19/51, SC Archives, microfilm reel MF-SF-SC-51.

105. SRD Minutes, RS 3466/60733, TX-G Committee to Distribution, dtd 5/31/51, subject, Minutes of the 7th Meeting. SC Reports Files.

106. SRD Ltr, RS 3421-4/2693, TX-G Committee to Sandia Corporation and Los Alamos Scientific Laboratory, dtd 6/23/51, subject, TX-11 Program. SC Archives, microfilm reel MF-SF-SC-29.

107. SRD Ltr, RS 1/144, Sandia Corporation and Los Alamos Scientific Laboratory to Santa Fe Operations Office, dtd 7/24/51, subject, Proposed Participation of BuOrd in Gun-Type Atomic Warhead Development Program. AEC Files, MRA, 9-1, TX-10, Volume I.

108. SRD Ltr, Division of Military Application to Military Liaison Committee, dtd 8/6/51, subject, TX-11 Program. AEC Files, MRA, Mk 8-10-11, 7/51-9/51.

UNCLASSIFIED

RS 3434/7

109. SRD Minutes, RS 3466/61301, TX-G Steering Committee to Distribution, dtd 1/24/52, subject, Minutes of 15th Meeting. SC Reports Files.

110. SRD Minutes, RS 3466/67126, TX-G Steering Committee to Distribution, dtd 6/19/52, subject, Minutes of 19th Meeting. SC Reports Files.

111. SRD Ltr, RS 1200/566, Sandia Corporation to Bureau of Ordnance, dtd 6/30/52, subject, Approval of TX-11 Shape. SC Archives, TX-11, Transfer No. 30331.

112.

(b)(3)

113.

114. SRD Ltr, RS 3421-4/2691, TX-G Committee to Sandia Corporation, dtd 6/29/51, subject, Gun-Type Penetrating Atomic Warhead. SC Archives, microfilm reel MF-SF-SC-29.

115. SRD Ltr, RS 3421-4/2073, Bureau of Ordnance to Santa Fe Operations Office, dtd 2/26/52, subject, Adaptation of Gun-Type Atomic Warheads to Guided Missiles. SC Archives, microfilm reel MF-SF-SC-103.

116. SRD Minutes, RS 3466/67184, TX-G Steering Committee to Distribution, dtd 6/21/52, subject, Minutes of 20th Meeting. SC Reports Files.

117. SRD Ltr, RS 1/420, Sandia Corporation and Los Alamos Scientific Laboratory to Division of Military Application, dtd 1/8/53, subject, TX-11 Development Schedule. SC Archives, TX-11, Transfer No. 30331.

118. SRD Ltr, Division of Military Application to Santa Fe Operations Office, dtd 4/21/53, subject, TX-11 Development and Production. AEC Files, MRA, Mk 8-10-11, 4/53-6/53.

119. SRD Minutes, RS 3466/68294, Special Weapons Development Board to Distribution, dtd 7/29/53, subject, Minutes of 74th Meeting. SC Archives, Transfer No. 48217.

120. SRD Ltr, Bureau of Ordnance to Field Command, dtd 6/2/54, subject, Project TX-11; Assignment of Mk Numbers to TX-11 Production Weapons. AEC Files, MRA, 9-1, TX-11, Volume III.

121.

122.   (b)(3)

THIS PAGE INTENTIONALLY BLANK

www.ingramcontent.com/pod-product-compliance
Lightning Source LLC
Chambersburg PA
CBHW050620110426
42813CB00010B/2624